PIANO SOLOS
CHRISTMAS JAZZ

ARRANGED BY FRANK MANTOOTH

CONTENTS

ISBN 0-7935-1772-9

 **Hal Leonard Publishing Corporation**
7777 West Bluemound Road P.O. Box 13819 Milwaukee, WI 53213

AULD LANG SYNE

Slowly, Retrospectively (♩ = 60)

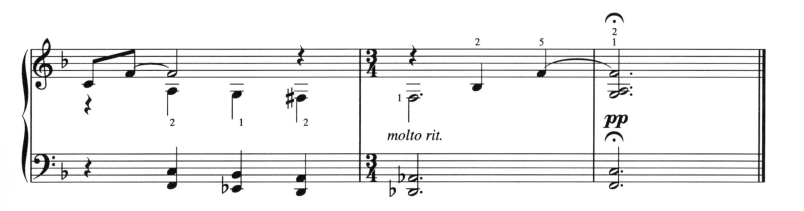

BRING A TORCH, JEANNETTE, ISABELLA

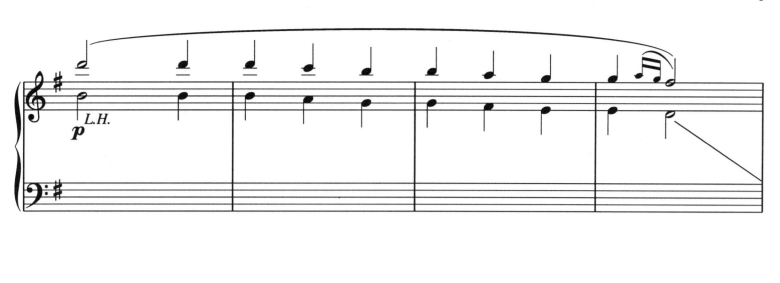

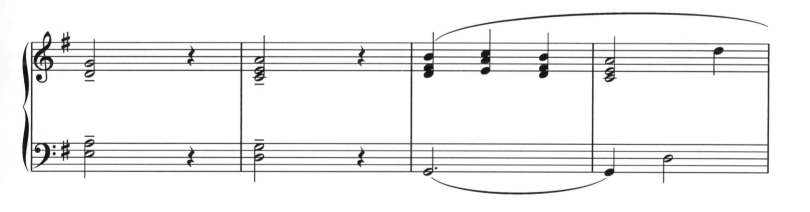

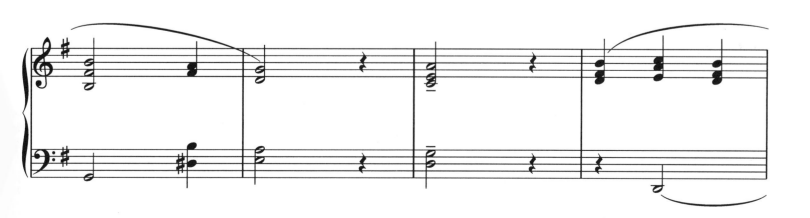

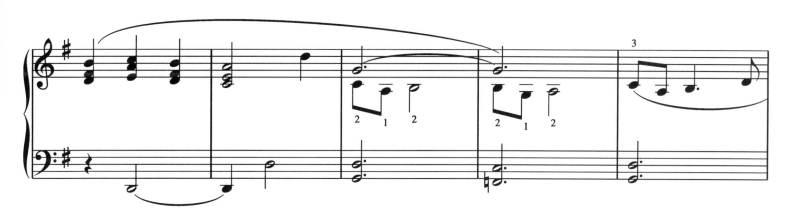

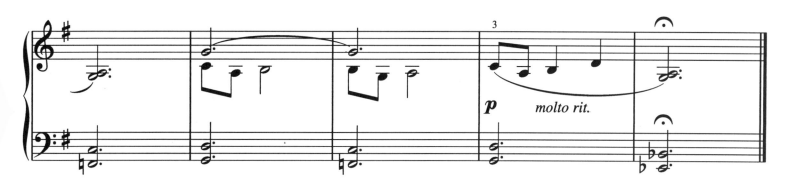

THE COVENTRY CAROL

In strict time (♩.= 60)

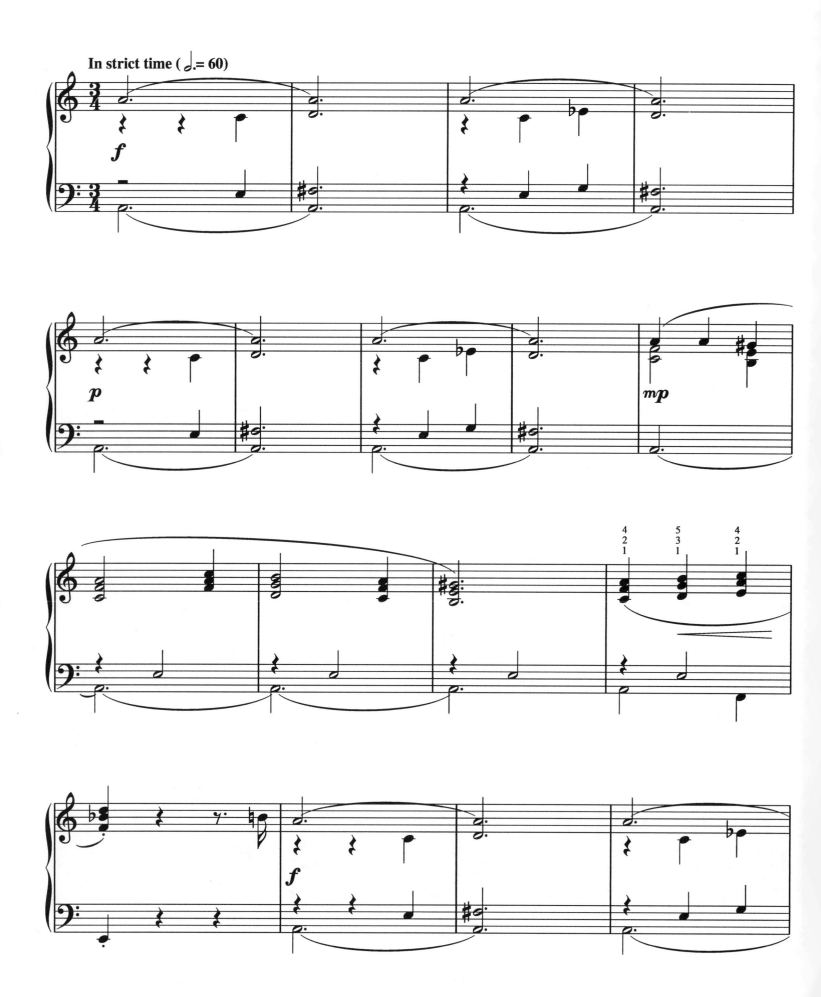

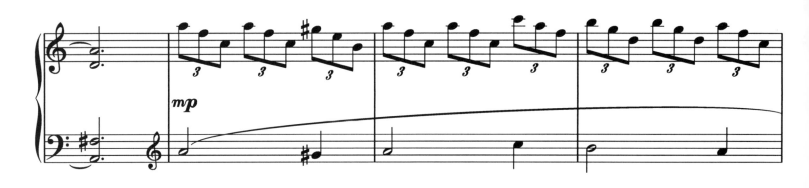

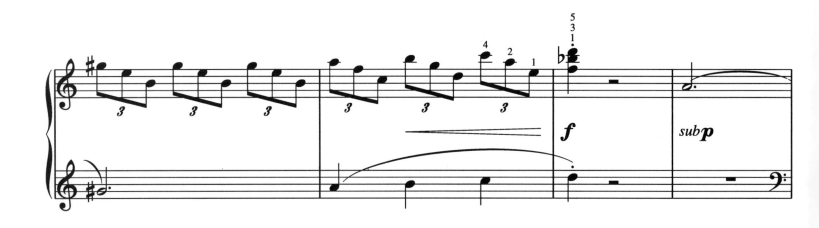

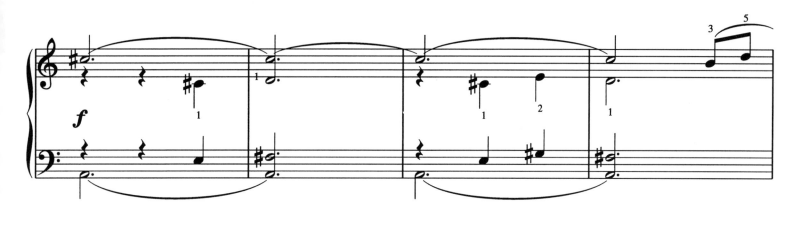

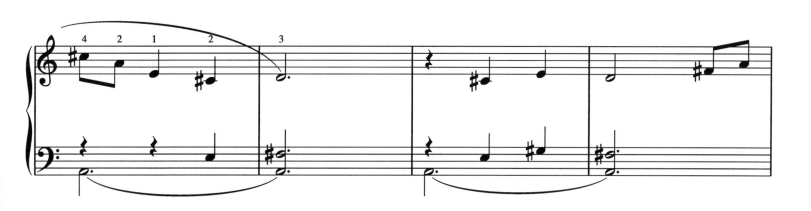

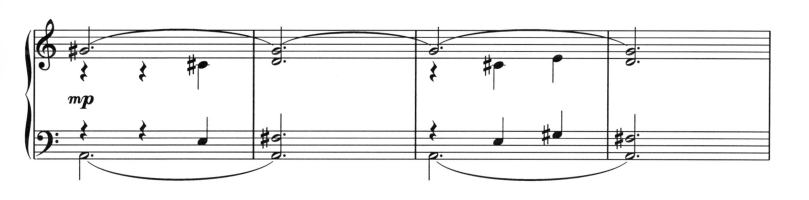

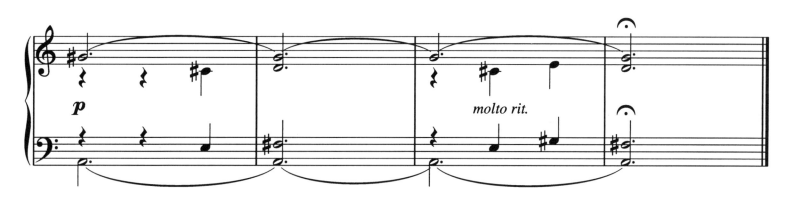

GO TELL IT ON THE MOUNTAIN

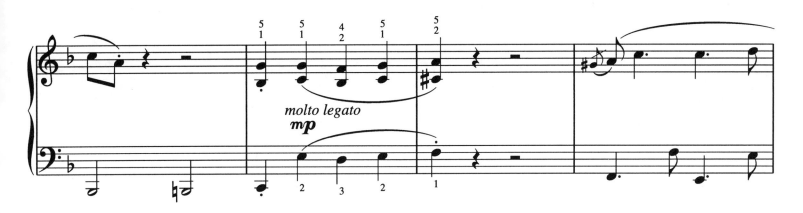

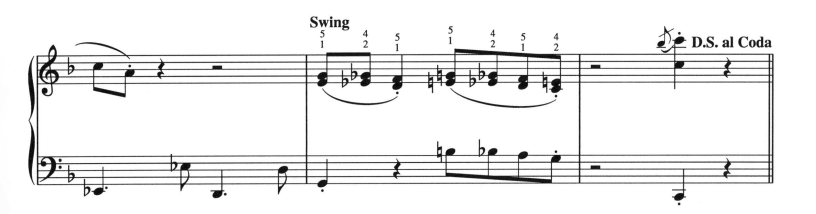

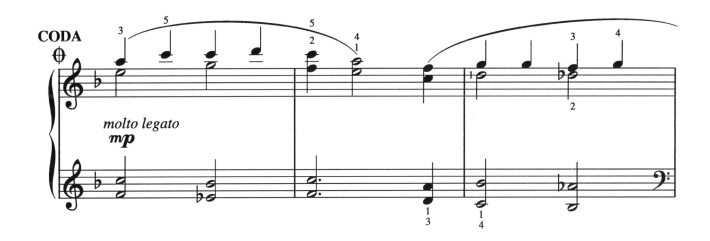

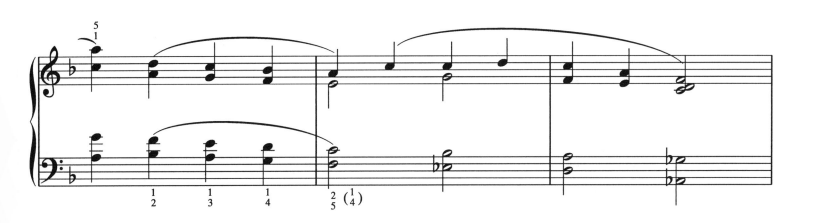

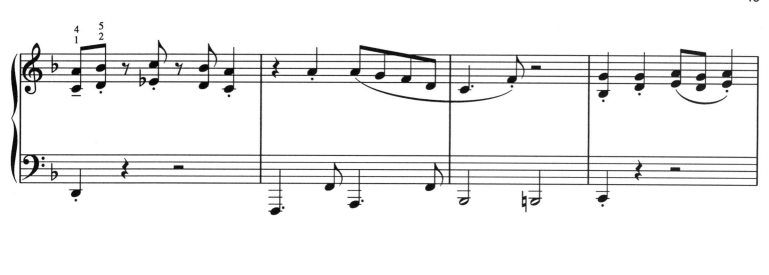

AWAY IN A MANGER

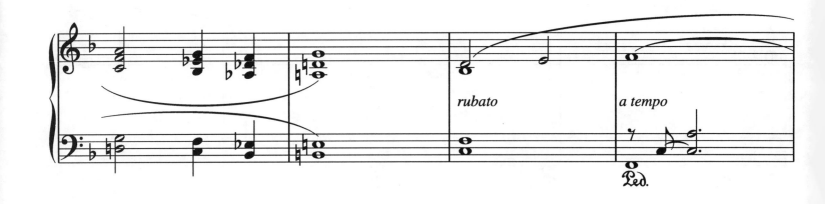

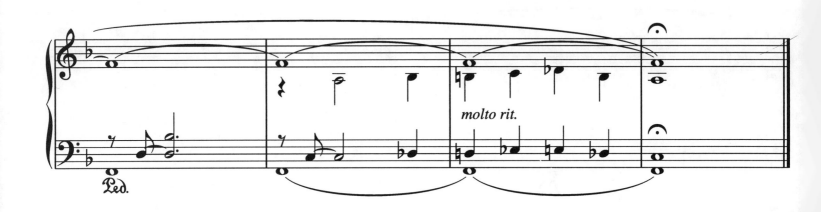

I HEARD THE BELLS
ON CHRISTMAS DAY

Slowly, but with a steady pulse ($\quad$ = 92)

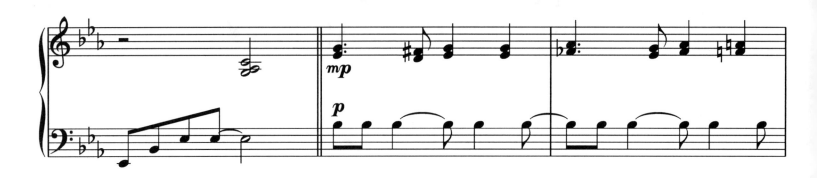

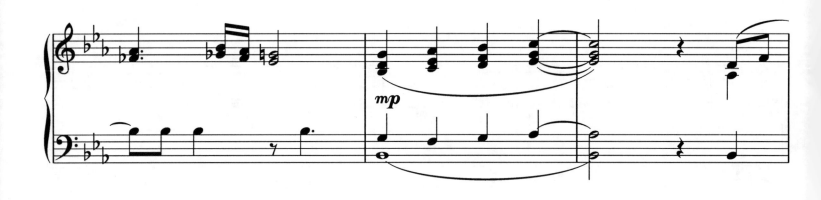

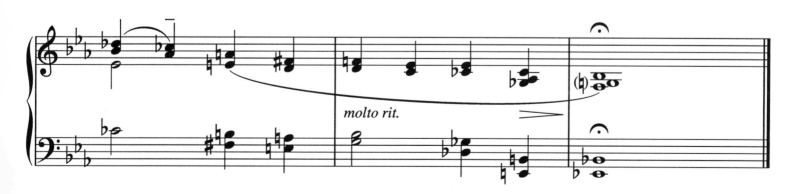

JINGLE BELLS

Easy bossa nova feel (♩ = 120)

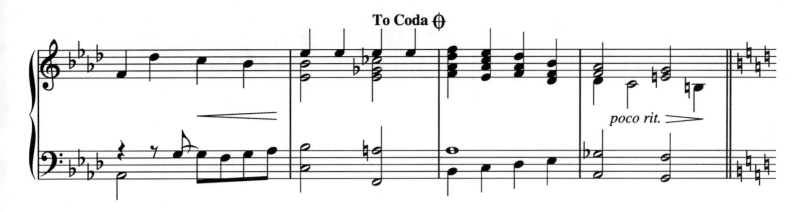

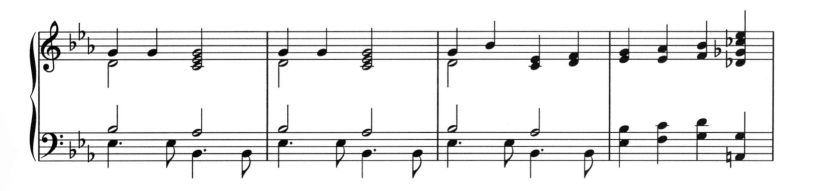

D.S. al Coda

CODA

f

p *molto legato*

JOLLY OLD ST. NICHOLAS

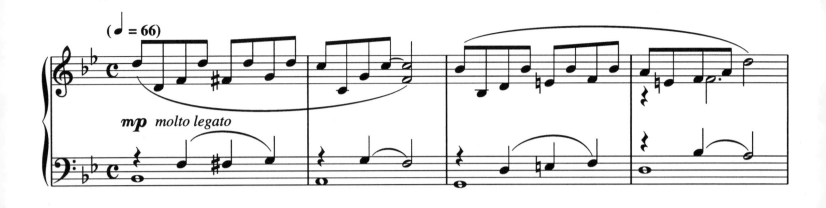

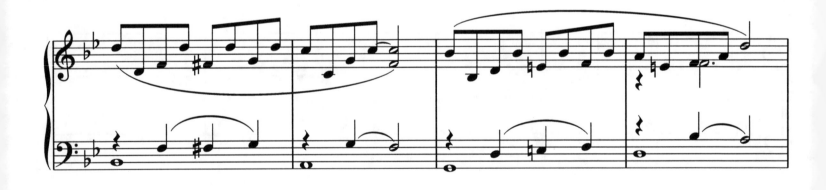

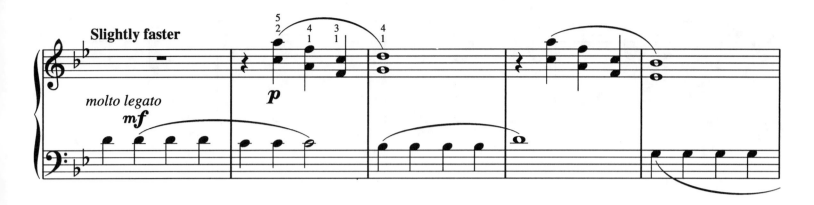

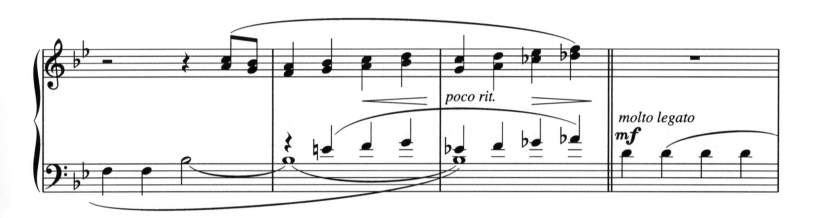

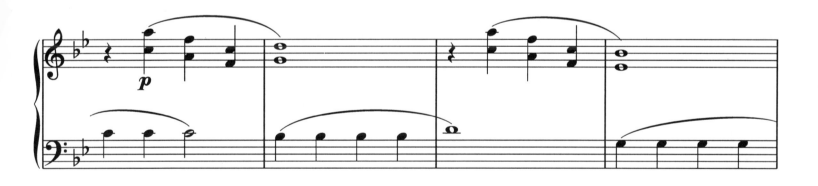

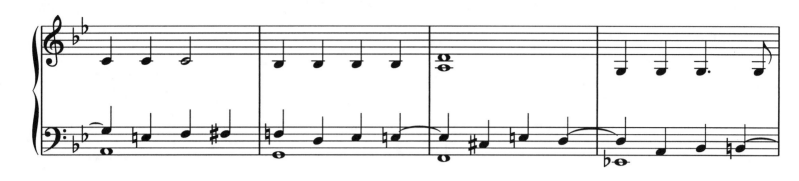

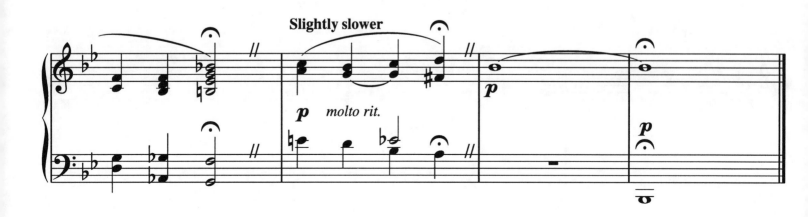

O COME, LITTLE CHILDREN

O CHRISTMAS TREE

SILENT NIGHT

36

TOYLAND

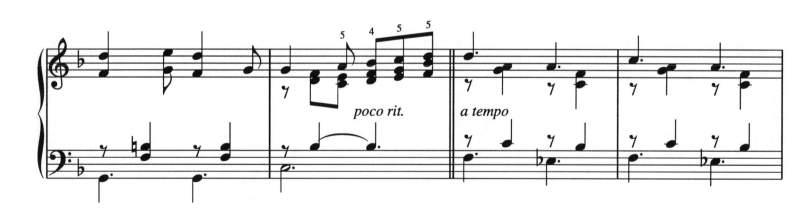

WE WISH YOU A MERRY CHRISTMAS

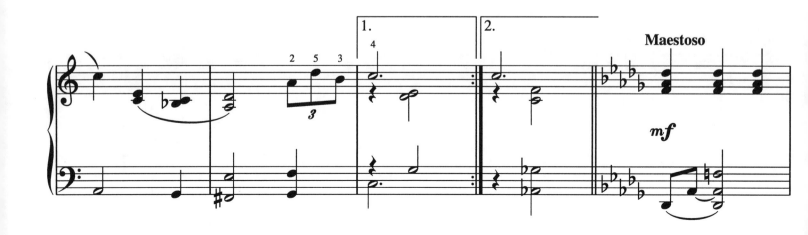

Tempo Primo

UP ON THE HOUSETOP

Strict tempo (♩=120)
a la music box

ff

p

poco rit.   *a tempo*

Boogie woogie (♩ = 144)

Frank Mantooth is currently active as a pianist, composer, arranger, clinician and educator residing in Oak Park, Illinois. Frank's first album for the Optimism label, "Suite Tooth", has been met with critical acclaim including a four-star review in the April, 1990 Down Beat, and Grammy nominations in three categories.

The release of his second album (Persevere) on the Optimism label featuring Pete Christlieb and Clark Terry has also been met with a glowing endorsement by the Jazz Times. As an author, Frank has recently published "The Best Chord Changes for the World's Greatest Standards", and "The Best Chord Changes For The Most Requested Standards," for Hal Leonard Publishing Corp. This is in addition to over 100 works for combo and jazz ensemble which have been published since 1978.

Recent writing commissions have come from Texas Tech University, The Army Blues, Doc Severinsen, Bobby Shew, Pete Christlieb, Louie Bellson, and the Airmen of Note.

Recently released on the Seabreeze label was Frank's latest recording project, "Dangerous Precedent" which features Ramsey Lewis and Clark Terry. "Christmas Jazz" is Frank's first anthology for solo piano.